WILDLIFE CONSERVATION

GLOBAL CITIZENS: ENVIRONMENTALISM

Published in the United States of America by Cherry Lake Publishing
Ann Arbor, Michigan
www.cherrylakepublishing.com

Content Adviser: Michael Rockett MS, Natural resources

Reading Adviser: Marla Conn MS, Ed., Literacy specialist, Read-Ability, Inc.

Photo Credits: © JLwarehouse / Shutterstock.com, cover, 1; © kojik / Shutterstock.com, 5; © Everett Historical / Shutterstock.
com, 6; © Dimitris Timpilis / Shutterstock.com, 8; © Rich Carey / Shutterstock.com, 10; © Kevin Wells Photography /
Shutterstock.com, 13; © Andrea Izzotti / Shutterstock.com, 14; ©ricardo del griotto / Shutterstock.com, 16; © GUDKOV
ANDREY / Shutterstock.com, 19; © Shane Gross / Shutterstock.com, 20; © Birdiegal / Shutterstock.com, 22; © Chameleons-
Eye / Shutterstock.com; © GUDKOV ANDREY / Shutterstock.com, 26; © a katz / Shutterstock.com, 28

Library of Congress Cataloging-in-Publication Data
Names: Labrecque, Ellen.
Title: Wildlife conservation / Ellen Labrecque.
Description: Ann Arbor : Cherry Lake Publishing, 2017. | Series: Global citizens: environmentalism |
    Audience: Grade 4 to 6. | Includes bibliographical references and index.
Identifiers: LCCN 2016058570| ISBN 9781634728669 (hardcover) | ISBN 9781534100442 (pbk.) |
    ISBN 9781634729550 (pdf) | ISBN 9781534101333 (hosted ebook)
Subjects: LCSH: Wildlife conservation—Juvenile literature.
Classification: LCC QL83 .L33 2017 | DDC 333.95/4—dc23
LC record available at https://lccn.loc.gov/2016058570

Cherry Lake Publishing would like to acknowledge the work of the Partnership for 21st Century Learning.
Please visit *www.p21.org* for more information.

Printed in the United States of America
Corporate Graphics

ABOUT THE AUTHOR

Ellen Labrecque has written over 100 books for children. She is passionate about being a friend to the environment and taking care of our planet. She lives in Pennsylvania with her husband, Jeff, and her two young "editors," Sam and Juliet. She loves running, hiking, and reading.

TABLE OF CONTENTS

CHAPTER 1

History: Earth's Animals

Environmentalism is a big word. But its meaning is simple. Practicing environmentalism means being a friend to Earth and all its creatures. Environmentalists want to keep our air healthy, our land clean, and our water fresh. They want to take care of our plants and animals by making sure our planet remains a safe place to live. Some environmentalists focus on encouraging people to stop polluting. Others encourage people to **recycle**. One of the most important environmental jobs is to protect our plants and animals. This type of environmentalism is called wildlife conservation.

Sea turtles are one of the many animals that are under special protection.

Theodore Roosevelt was the 26th president of the United States.

The Story of Wildlife Conservation

Conservationists work to help plants and animals live safely in their own **habitats**. Conservationists do this by making sure the plants and animals have the right food, water, and shelter needed to survive. They protect plants and animals living in forests, marshes, grasslands, beaches, ponds, rivers, and oceans.

For centuries, animals and plants lived freely and thrived in the wild. But our human **population** grew and grew. In the 1800s, there were one billion people in the world. Today, that number has increased to over 7 billion. People need food, water, and space to live. But animals need these things, too. Today, environmentalists are urging people to share these resources and this space. They encourage people to build cities, neighborhoods, and roads without greatly affecting the homes of animals. But this can be hard.

As time went on, people began to understand that if we didn't change our ways, animals would suffer the most. Some animals went **extinct**. In 1901, Theodore Roosevelt became president of the United States. He created the US Forest Service (USFS) and passed the first laws to protect plants and animals. This **agency** made sure animals, plants, and trees could live in peace.

These birds are playing in the J.N. "Ding" Darling National Wildlife Refuge in Florida.

Roosevelt also created the first national wildlife **refuge**, Pelican Island, off the coast of Florida. Egrets and other birds live there without the threat of being hunted or harmed.

Getting Organized

In 1936, the National Wildlife Federation was created in the United States. An environmental cartoonist named Jay Norwood "Ding" Darling started the organization. He helped set up 3 million acres (1.2 million hectares) of land as wildlife refuges in North America.

Developing Questions

Why do some people refuse to wear animal fur or leather? In what ways would this help protect wild animals? What are other ways you can help wild animals?

A close-ended question is a question that can be answered with a simple yes or no. An open-ended question is one that needs more thought when answering. The questions above are open-ended questions. They are meant to make you think about ways you can help animals rather than just answering yes or no.

Deforestation is an environmental problem.

In 1961, scientists and animal lovers started the World Wildlife Fund (WWF), with headquarters in Switzerland. One of the first things WWF did was set up reserves, or areas of protected land, for tigers all over the world. **Deforestation** left many tigers with no place to live. Many of them were already being hunted and killed for their fur. Some **species** of tigers were even becoming **endangered**. Over the last century, the tiger population has gone from more than 100,000 to just 3,890 today.

The reserves have helped save some of these big cats. For the first time in more than 100 years, the wild tiger population has started to increase, after years of decline.

CHAPTER 2

Geography: Helping Wild Animals Everywhere

Animal refuges can be found all over the world. Conservationists draw a boundary, like a giant invisible line, around a certain area, to create a refuge. It is meant to be a safe zone for animals. For instance, inside refuges, people can't tear down trees or plants, build structures, or hunt.

In the United States, there are more than 560 national wildlife refuges—at least one in every US state and territory. These refuges are home to more than 700 types of birds, 220 varieties of mammals, 250 kinds of reptiles and amphibians, and 1,000 species of fish!

This masked tree frog makes its home in a wildlife refuge in Costa Rica.

Over 900 endangered Hawaiian monk seals live in Papahānaumokuākea
Marine National Monument.

Papahānaumokuākea Marine National Monument is the world's largest wildlife refuge. It is made up of over 135,000 square miles (over 350,000 square kilometers) in the Pacific Ocean and includes 10 small islands and coral reefs. More than 7,000 different species live here safely.

Room to Roam

Refuges are a great way to keep wild animals safe. But some scientists believe there is another way to keep them safe, too. Some conservationists want to create a long path along 5,000 miles (8,047 km) of the Rocky Mountains, from Canada

Gathering and Evaluating Sources

Different types of maps show different things. A political map shows the borders of countries and states. Physical maps show landscape features, such as mountains and rivers. Conservationists use habitat maps. Habitat maps show where different types of wildlife live in a region such as a state or country. Knowing where wildlife is aids environmentalists in helping to protect them and their homes.

Grizzly bears were once endangered, but efforts were made to increase their safety.

to New Mexico, that would allow animals to roam free. They want to call this the first "wildway" in the United States. This wildway would allow a way for animals, like grizzly bears and wolves, to safely **migrate** higher into the mountains. This project is called "The Spine of the Continent." It will protect the routes that allow animals to get where they need to go.

Wildlife Refuges

Wildlife refuges can be found all over the world. You can visit many of them. On the Web site of the National Wildlife Refuge System, you can search the closest one to your home. To look for a refuge near you, go to www.fws.gov/refuges.

CHAPTER 3

Civics: Everybody Helps

Different governments around the world, as well as private organizations, do the work of wildlife conservation. Both sides work together to help wildlife.

Government

Governments around the world have an important job to do for wildlife. They establish laws and policies that protect wildlife, water, air, and land. If there were no laws limiting where people can build and hunt, wildlife would suffer. Government officials create the laws telling people what they can and cannot do. They do this work in their own countries, but they also work together with governments around the world.

People are hunting cheetahs into extinction.

In 2010, leaders from 200 countries met to talk about wildlife conservation. Together, they pledged to increase wildlife refuge areas from 1 to 13 percent of the world's oceans and from 10 to 17 percent of land.

Government laws also make the hunting of some wild animals illegal. In 1973, the US government passed the Endangered Species Act. This act protects wild animals that are in danger of becoming extinct. For instance, blue whales are listed as endangered species. They were hunted for years for their fat,

Sperm whales were also hunted for their oil.

which can be turned into oil for lamps and cooking. Under this new law, it is illegal to hunt and kill them. Buying or selling whales is also illegal.

People Making a Difference

WWF was started not by governments, but by individuals who wanted to help animals. The organization declared, "All over the world today, vast numbers of fine and harmless creatures are losing their lives or their homes." WWF's primary mission is to stop this. And since the beginning, it has saved countless animals. In China, WWF helped establish 62 national reserves to

Developing Claims and Using Evidence

Some people think hunting animals is okay for food and for sport. Other people don't think any animals should be hunted. Do some research using the Internet and your local library. Can you find evidence supporting hunting and evidence against hunting? Using evidence you find, form your own opinion on this subject.

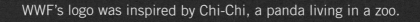
WWF's logo was inspired by Chi-Chi, a panda living in a zoo.

protect pandas. In mountain areas all over Asia, it set up refuges to protect the snow leopards. WWF has also tried to protect rhinoceroses, which are poached, or hunted, for their horns.

Many people work hard to protect wildlife on their own. Alan Rabinowitz is a wildlife zoologist. He explores some of Earth's wildest places while working to protect the world's biggest cats, like lions, jaguars, and tigers. Rabinowitz also started the conservation group Panthera. Panthera creates protected areas for snow leopards in the Himalayas and refuges for lions across Africa.

CHAPTER 4

Economics: Funding for Wildlife

Governments and private organizations spend billions of dollars a year on wildlife conservation. This money is used to save endangered species and protect their habitats. Conservationists believe the cost is worth saving our wildlife. Where exactly does this money go?

Research

Conservationists travel all over the world to learn about different animals and how they live. When conservationists travel, they usually talk to the people who live in the areas where the wild animals are. They teach people how they can live in harmony with the species around them.

This Australian conservationist is teaching people about the barking owl.

Wildlife refuges create safe homes for many animals, like gorillas.

Getting the Word Out

It is important to learn which animals are endangered. This way, people will donate their time and money to help the animals survive. Building Web sites, writing books, and making television shows and movies can help teach people about the risks of doing nothing.

Establishing Wildlife Refuges

The most important work of wildlife conservation is setting up refuges—places where these animals can live safely in their own habitat. It costs money to buy and preserve this land as well as maintain the land once it is established as a refuge.

Taking Informed Action

Do you want to support wildlife conservation? There are many ways you can get involved and many different organizations you can explore. Here are three to check out:

- Save the Elephants: Learn about how this organization secures safe places for elephants all over the world.
- WildAid: Discover how this organization stops the buying and selling of illegal animals and animal products.
- American Birding Association: Find out how to protect wild birds.

Park rangers and conservationists teach people how to care for wildlife.

Communicating Conclusions

Before reading this book, did you know about wildlife conservation? Now that you know more, why do you think this is an important issue? Share your knowledge about animal refuges and the importance of being a friend to all of Earth's creatures. Every week, look up different organizations that support wildlife. Share what you learn with friends at school or with family at home.

Wildlife Conservation Makes Money for People

Wildlife conservation also brings money and jobs into countries. Many people like to live close to nature. Homes become more valuable when they are near animal refuges. One US study done in 2012 showed that 14 refuges in the Southeast added $122 million to local property values in one year. Every year, 47 million Americans visit refuges, generating $1.7 billion that goes into the economy. Tourists spend money on things such as hotels and restaurants. Jobs are created. Over 3,000 people work for wildlife refuges in the United States.

Think About It

Biologists estimate there are about 8.7 million species on Earth. Of these species, over 23,000 are on the endangered list and face possible extinction. In the past 500 years, over 1,000 species have all gone extinct. Scientists think this mass extinction is happening so rapidly, it will rival what happened to the dinosaurs 65 million years ago. Why do you think saving wildlife is important? What are ways we can help protect these animals? Use your local library and the Internet to gather information. Support your argument with the data you find.

For More Information

FURTHER READING

Goddard, Donald, and Sam Swope, eds. *Saving Wildlife: A Century of Conservation*. New York: Harry N. Abrams, 1995.

McGrath, Susan. *Saving Our Animal Friends*. Washington DC: National Geographic Society, 1986.

Scardina, Julie, and Jeff Flocken. *Wildlife Heroes: 40 Leading Conservationists and the Animals They Are Committed to Saving.* Philadelphia: Running Press, 2012.

WEB SITES

National Wildlife Federation
www.nwf.org
Find out about wildlife conservation in the United States.

World Wildlife Fund
www.worldwildlife.org
This is a great place to begin your wildlife conservation research.

GLOSSARY

agency (AY-juhn-see) a government department that provides a service to the public

conservationists (kahn-sur-VAY-shuhn-ists) people who work to save and conserve Earth and all the life on it

deforestation (dee-for-is-TAY-shuhn) the act of clearing out all the trees in a forest

endangered (en-DAYN-jurd) at risk of becoming extinct

environmentalism (en-vye-ruhn-MEN-tuhl-iz-uhm) working to protect the air, water, animals, and plants from pollution and other harmful things

extinct (ik-STINGT) no longer exists or has died out

habitats (HAB-i-tats) the natural environments or homes of animals

migrate (MYE-grate) to go from one country, region, or climate to another

population (pahp-yuh-LAY-shuhn) the number of people in one place

recycle (ree-SYE-kuhl) to break something down in order to make something new from it

refuge (REF-yooj) a place of safety for animals to live

species (SPEE-sheez) a group of animals that are the same type or breed

INDEX